Thomas Kinkade
Painter of Light™

The Lord's Prayer

Thomas Kinkade Studios
HarperCollinsPublishers
A Parachute Press Book

The Lord's Prayer
All artwork © 2006 by Thomas Kinkade Studios, Morgan Hill, CA
A Parachute Press Book

Manufactured in China.

For information address HarperCollins Children's Books, a division of
HarperCollins Publishers, 1350 Avenue of the Americas, New York, NY 10019.
www.harperchildrens.com

Library of Congress Cataloging-in-Publication Data
The Lord's prayer / [illustrated by] Thomas Kinkade.— 1st ed.
     p.   cm.
"A Parachute Press book."
ISBN-10: 0-06-078738-4 (trade bdg.) — ISBN-13: 978-0-06-078738-7 (trade bdg.)
ISBN-10: 0-06-078739-2 (lib. bdg.) — ISBN-13: 978-0-06-078739-4 (lib. bdg.)
1. Lord's prayer—Illustrations. I. Kinkade, Thomas, 1958-
BV230.L557 2006   2005018899
226.9'6052034—dc22   CIP
                                                                                      AC

Typography by Jeanne L. Hogle
1 2 3 4 5 6 7 8 9 10

First Edition

*T*he Lord's Prayer is the first prayer I can remember learning as a child. I don't think I recognized all the words back then, but somehow I understood their meaning. My favorite words were the first two, "Our Father." They went right to a child's heart and offered peace and comfort.

Years later, as I taught the prayer to my own children, it took on new meanings. Now it spoke to me of responsibility and of doing right. It offered the familiar feelings of comfort and peace, along with a new sense of serenity.

The prayer continues to grow in essence for me as I grow in years. In this book I have chosen to go beyond the literal meaning of the words of the Lord's Prayer. Instead the images created by the Thomas Kinkade Studios convey the glory of God's earth and the joy and promise of everlasting life in his grace. I offer it to you to share with your family as I share it with mine.

Thomas Kinkade

THOMAS KINKADE

Our Father, who art in heaven,

Hallowed be thy name.

Thy kingdom come.

Thy will be done,

On earth as it is in heaven.

Give us this day our daily bread.

And forgive us our trespasses,
    As we forgive those who trespass against us.

And lead us not into temptation,
But deliver us from evil.

For thine is the kingdom, and the power,
and the glory,

For ever and ever.
Amen.

Our Father, who art in heaven,
Hallowed be thy name.
Thy kingdom come.
Thy will be done,
On earth as it is in heaven.

Give us this day our daily bread.
And forgive us our trespasses,
As we forgive those who trespass against us.
And lead us not into temptation,
But deliver us from evil.
For thine is the kingdom, and the power, and the glory,
For ever and ever.
Amen.